MISCELLANEOUS SKETCHES

MORE WILDSIDE CLASSICS

MISCELLANEOUS SKETCHES

NELLIE BLY

WILDSIDE PRESS

MISCELLANEOUS SKETCHES

This edition published in 2009 by Wildside Press, LLC.
www.wildsidebooks.com

MISCELLANEOUS
SKETCHES

CONTENTS

TRYING TO BE A SERVANT

MY STRANGE EXPERIENCE AT TWO EMPLOYMENT AGENCIES

NONE but the initiated know what a great question the servant question is and how many perplexing sides it has. The mistresses and servants, of course, fill the leading *roles*. Then, in the lesser, but still important parts, come the agencies, which despite the many voices clamoring against them, declare themselves public benefactors. Even the "funny man" manages to fill a great deal of space with the subject. It is a serious question, since it affects all one holds dear in life — one's dinner, one's bed, and one's linen. I had heard so many complaints from long-suffering mistresses, worked-out servants, agencies, and lawyers, that I determined to investigate the subject to my own satisfaction. There was only one way to do it. That was to personate a servant and apply for a situation. I knew that there might be such things as "references" required, and, as I had never tested my abilities in this line, I did not know how to furnish them. Still, it would not do to allow a little thing like a "reference " to stop me in my work, and I would not ask any friend to commit herself to further my efforts. Many girls must at one time be without references, I thought, and this encouraged me to make the risk.

On Monday afternoon a letter came to the *World*

office from a lawyer, complaining of an agency where, he claimed, a client of his had paid for a servant, and the agent then refused to produce a girl. This shop I decided to make my first essay. Dressed to look the character I wanted to represent, I walked up Fourth Avenue until I found No. 69, the place I wanted. It was a low frame building which retained all the impressions of old age. The room on the first floor was filled with a conglomeration of articles which gave it the appearance of a second-hand store. By a side door, leaning against the wall, was a large sign which told the passing public that that was the entrance to the "Germania Servants' Agency." On a straight, blue board, fastened lengthwise to a second-story window, was, in large, encouraging white letters, the ominous word "Servants."

I entered the side door, and as there was nothing before me but the dirty, uncarpeted hall and a narrow, rickety-looking staircase, I went on to my fate. I passed two closed doors on the first landing, and on the third I saw the word "Office." I did not knock, but turned the knob of the door, and, as it stuck top and bottom, I pressed my shoulder against it. It gave way, so did I, and I entered on my career as a servant with a tumble. It was a small room, with a low ceiling, a dusty ingrain carpet and cheaply papered walls. A heavy railing and a high desk and counter which divided the room gave it the appearance of a police court. Around the walls were hung colored advertisements of steamship lines and maps. Above the mantel, which was decorated with two plaster-of-Paris busts, was a square sheet of white paper. I viewed the large black letters on this paper with a quaking heart. "REFERENCES INVESTIGATED!!" with two exclamation points. Now, if it had only been put quietly and mildly, or even with one exclamation point, but two   dreadful. It was a death warrant to the idea I had of writing my own references if any were demanded.

A young woman who was standing with a downcast head by the window turned to look at the abrupt newcomer. A man who had apparently been conversing with her came hastily forward to the desk. He was a middle-sized man, with a sharp, gray eye, a bald head, and a black frock-coat buttoned up tightly, showing to disadvantage his rounded shoulders.

"Well?" he said to me, in a questioning manner, as he glanced quickly over my "get up."

"Are you the man who gets places for girls?" I asked, as if there were but one such man.

"Yes, I'm the man. Do you want a place?" he asked, with a decidedly German twang.

"Yes, I want a place," I replied.

"What did you work at last?"

"Oh, I was a chambermaid. Can you get me a position, do you think?"

"Yes, I can do that," he replied. "You're a nice-looking girl and I can soon get you a place. Just the other day I got a girl a place for $20 a month, just because she was nice-looking. Many gentlemen, and ladies also, will pay more when girls are nice-looking. Where did you work last?"

"I worked in Atlantic City," I replied, with a mental cry for forgiveness.

"Have you no city references?"

"No, none whatever; but I want a job in this city, that's why I came here."

"Well, I can get you a position, never fear, only some people are mighty particular about references."

"Have you no place you can send me to now?" I said, determined to get at my business as soon as possible.

"You have to pay to get your name entered on the book first," he said, opening a large ledger as he asked, "What is your name?"

"How much do you charge?" I asked, in order to give me time to decide on a name.

"I charge you one dollar for the use of the bureau for a month, and if I get you a big salary you will have to pay more."

"How much more?"

"That depends entirely on your salary," he answered, non-committal. "Your name?"

"Now, if I give you a dollar you will assure me a situation?"

"Certainly, that's what I'm here for."

"And you guarantee me work in this city?" I urged.

"Oh, certainly, certainly; that's what this agency is for. I'll get you a place, sure enough."

"All right, I'll give you a dollar, which is a great deal for a girl out of work. My name is Sally Lees."

"What shall I put you down for?" he asked.

"Oh, anything," I replied, with a generosity that surprised myself.

"Then I shall put it chambermaid, waitress, nurse or seamstress."

So my name, or the one assumed, was entered in the ledger, and as I paid my dollar, I ventured the information that if he gave me a situation directly I should be pleased to give him more money. He warmed up at this and told me he should advertise me in the morning.

"Then you have no one in want of help now?"

"We have plenty of people, but not just now. They all come in the morning. This is too late in the day. Where are you boarding?"

At this moment a woman clad in a blue dress, with a small, black shawl wrapped around her, entered from a room in the rear. She also looked me over sharply, as if I was an article for sale, as the man told her in German all that he knew about me.

"You can stay here," she said, in broken, badly broken English, after she had learned that I was friendless in the city. "Where is your baggage?"

"I left my baggage where I paid for my lodging tonight," I answered. They tried to induce me to stop at their house. Only $2.50 a week, with board, or 20 cents a night for a bed. They urged that it was immaterial to them, only I had a better chance to secure work if I was always there; it was only for my own good they suggested it. I had one glance of the adjoining bedroom, and that sight made me firm in my determination to sleep elsewhere.

As the evening drew on I felt they would have no more applications for servants that afternoon, and after asking the hour that I should return in the morning, I requested a receipt for my money. "You don't need to be so particular," he said, crossly, but I told him I was and insisted until he was forced to comply. It was not much of a receipt. He wrote on the blank side of the agency's advertising card:

"Sally Lees has paid $1. Good for one month use of bureau. 69 4th Ave."

* * * *

ON the following morning, about 10:30, I made my appearance at the agency. Some eight or ten girls were in the room and the man who had pocketed my fee on the previous afternoon still adorned the throne back of the desk. No one said good-morning, or anything else for that matter, so I quietly slid onto a chair near the door. The girls were all comfortably dressed, and looked as if they had enjoyed hearty breakfasts. All sat silent, with a dreamy expression on their faces, except two who stood by the window watching the passing throng and conversing in whispers with one another. I wanted to be with or near them, so that I might hear what was said. After waiting for some time I decided to awake the man to the fact that I wanted work, not a rest.

"Have you no place to send me this morning?"

"No; but I advertised you in the paper," and he handed me the *Tribune* of October 25 and pointed out the following notice:

> "NURSE, &c. — By excellent, very neat English girl as nurse and seamstress, chambermaid and waitress, or parlor maid. Call at 69 4th ave.; no cards answered."

I choked down a laugh as I read myself advertised in this manner and wondered what my *rôle* would be the next time. I began to hope some one would soon call for the excellent girl, but when an aged gentleman entered I wished just as fervently that he was not after me. I was enjoying my position too much, and I fear I could not restrain my gravity if any one began to question me. Poor old gentleman! He looked around helplessly, as if he was at a loss to know what to do. The agent did not leave him long in doubt. "You want a girl, sir?"

"Yes, my wife read an advertisement in the *Tribune* this morning, and she sent me here to see the girl."

"Yes, yes, excellent girl, sir, come right back here," opening the gates and giving the gentleman a chair behind the high counter. "You come here, Sally Lees," indicating a chair beside the visitor for me. I sat down with an inward chuckle, and the agent leaned over the back of a chair. The visitor eyed me nervously, and after clearing his throat several times and making vain attempts at a beginning, he said:

"You are the girl who wants work?" And after I answered in the affirmative, he said: "Of course you know how to do all these things — you know what is required of a girl?"

"Oh, yes, I know," I answered confidently.

"Yes — well, how much do you want a month?"

"Oh, anything," I answered, looking to the agent for aid. He understood the look, for he began hurriedly:

"Fourteen dollars a month, sir. She is an excellent girl, good, neat, quick and of an amiable disposition."

I was astonished at his knowledge of my good qualities, but I maintained a lofty silence.

"Yes, yes," the visitor said, musingly. "My wife only pays ten dollars a month, and then if the girl is all right she is willing to pay more, you know. I really couldn't, you know —"

"We have no ten-dollar-girls here, sir," said the agent with dignity; "you can't get an honest, neat, and respectable girl for that amount."

"H'm, yes; well, this girl has good references, I suppose?"

"Oh, yes; I know all about her," said the agent, briskly and confidently. "She is an excellent girl, and I can give you the best personal reference — the best of references."

Here I was, unknown to the agent. So far as he knew, I might be a confidence woman, a thief, or everything wicked; and yet the agent was vowing that he had good personal references.

"Well, I live in Bloomfield, New Jersey, and there are only four in the family. Of course, you are a good washer and ironer?" he said, turning to me.

Before I had time to assure him of my wonderful skill in that line, the agent interposed:

"This is not the girl you want. No, sir, this girl won't do general housework. This is the girl you are after," bringing up another. "She does general housework," and he went on with a long list of her virtues, which were similar to those he had professed to find in me. The visitor got very nervous and began to insist that he could not take a girl unless his wife saw her first. Then the agent, when he found it impossible to make him take a girl, tried to induce the gentleman to join the bureau.

"It will only cost you $2 for the use of the bureau for a month," he urged, but the visitor began to get more nervous and to make his way to the door. I thought he was frightened because it was an agency, and it amused me to hear how earnestly he pleaded that really he dare not employ a girl without his wife's consent.

After the escape of this visitor we all resumed our former positions and waited for another visitor. It came in the shape of a red-haired Irish girl.

"Well, you are back again?" was the greeting given her.

"Yes. That woman was horrible. She and her husband fought all the time, and the cook carried tales to the mistress. Sure and I wouldn't live at such a place. A splendid laundress, with a good 'karacter,' don't need to stay in such places, I told them. The lady of the house made me wash every other day; then she wanted me to be dressed like a lady, sure, and wear a cap while I was at work. Sure and it's no good laundress who can be dressed up while at work, so I left her."

THE storm had scarcely passed when another girl with fiery locks entered. She had a good face and a bright one, and I watched her closely.

"So you are back, too. You are troublesome," said the agent.

Her eyes flashed as she replied:

"Oh, I'm troublesome, am I? Well, you can take a poor girl's money, anyway, and then you tell her she's troublesome. It wasn't troublesome when you took my money; and where is the position? I have walked all over the city, wearing out my shoes and spending my money in car-fare. Now, is this how you treat poor girls?"

"I did not mean anything by saying you were troublesome. That was only my fun," the agent tried to explain; and after awhile the girl quieted down.

Another girl came and was told that as she had not made her appearance the day previous she could not expect to obtain a situation. He refused to send her word if there was any chance.

Then a messenger boy called and said that Mrs.

Vanderpool, of No. 36 West Thirty-ninth Street, wanted the girl advertised in the morning paper. Irish girl No. 1 was sent, and she returned, after several hours' absence, to say that Mrs. Vanderpool said, when she learned where the girl came from, that she knew all about agencies and their schemes, and she did not propose to have a girl from them. The girl buttoned Mrs. Vanderpool's shoes and returned to the agency to take her post of waiting.

I succeeded at last in drawing one of the girls, Winifred Friel, into conversation. She said she had been waiting for several days, and that she had no chance of a place yet. The agency had a place out of town to which they tried to force girls who declared they would not leave the city. Quite strange, they never offered the place to girls who said they would work anywhere. Winifred Friel wanted it, but they would not allow her to go, yet they tried to insist on *me* accepting it.

"Well, now, if you won't take that, I would like to see you get a place this winter," he said, angrily, when he found that I would not go out of the city.

"Why, you promised that you would find me a situation in the city."

"That's no difference; if you won't take what I offer, you can do without," he said indifferently.

"Then give me back my money," I said.

"No, you can't have your money. That goes into the bureau."

I urged and insisted, to no avail, and so I left the agency, to return no more.

MY second day I decided to apply to another agency, so I went to Mrs. L. Seely's, No. 68 Twenty-second

Street. I paid my dollar fee and was taken to the third story and put in a small room which was packed as close with women as sardines in a box. After edging my way in, I was unable to move, so packed were we. A woman came up, and, calling me "that tall girl," told me roughly as I was new it was useless for me to wait there. Some of the girls said Mrs. Seely was always cross to them, and that I should not mind it.

How horribly stifling those rooms were! There were fifty-two people in the room with me, and the two other rooms I could look into were equally crowded, while groups stood on the stairs and in the hallway. It was a novel insight I got of life.

Some girls laughed, others were sad, some slept, some ate, and others read, while all sat from morning till night waiting a chance to earn a living. They are long waits too. One girl had been there two months, others for days and weeks. It was good to see the glad look when called out to see a lady, and sad to see them return saying that they did not suit because they wore bangs, or their hair in the wrong style, or that they looked bilious, or that they were too tall, too short, too heavy, or too slender. One poor woman could not obtain a place because she wore mourning, and so the objections ran.

I got no chance the entire day, and I decided that I could not endure a second day in that human pack for two situations, so framing some sort of excuse, I left the place and gave up trying to be a servant.

NELLIE BLY AS A WHITE SLAVE

HER EXPERIENCE IN THE ROLE OF A NEW YORK SHOP-GIRL MAKING PAPER BOXES

VERY EARLY the other morning, I started out, not with the pleasure-seekers, but with those who toil the day long that they may live. Everybody was rushing — girls of all ages and appearances and hurrying men — and I went along, as one of the throng. I had often wondered at the tales of poor pay and cruel treatment that working girls tell. There was one way of getting at the truth, and I determined to try it. It was becoming myself a paper box factory girl. Accordingly, I started out in search of work without experience, reference, or aught to aid me.

It was a tiresome search, to say the least. Had my living depended on it, it would have been discouraging, almost maddening. I went to a great number of factories in and around Bleecker and Grand streets and Sixth Avenue, where the workers number up into the hundreds.

"Do you know how to do the work?" was the question asked by every one. When I replied that I did not, they gave me no further attention.

"I am willing to work for nothing until I learn," I urged.

"Work for nothing! Why, if you paid us for coming, we wouldn't have you in our way," said one.

"We don't run an establishment to teach women trades," said another, in answer to my plea for work.

"Well, as they are not born with the knowledge, how do they ever learn?" I asked.

"The girls always have some friend who wants to learn. If she wishes to lose time and money by teaching her, we don't object, for we get the work the beginner does for nothing."

By no persuasion could I obtain an entree into the larger factories, so I concluded at last to try a smaller one at No. 196 Elm Street. Quite unlike the unkind, brusque men I had met at other factories, the man here was very polite.

He said: "If you have never done the work, I don't think you will like it. It is dirty work, and a girl has to spend years at it before she can make much money. Our beginners are girls about sixteen years old, and they do not get paid for two weeks after they come here."

"What can they make afterward?"

"We sometimes start them at week work — $1.50 a week. When they become competent they go on piece-work — that is, they are paid by the hundred."

"How much do they earn then?"

"A good worker will earn from $5 to $9 a week."

"Have you many girls here?"

"We have about sixty in the building and a number who take work home. I have only been in this business for a few months, but if you think you would like to try it, I shall speak to my partner. He has had some of his girls for eleven years. Sit down until I find him."

He left the office, and I soon heard him talking out-side about me, and rather urging that I be given a chance. He soon returned, and with him a small man who spoke with a German accent. He stood by me without speaking, so I repeated by request.

"Well, give your name to the gentleman at the desk, and come down on Monday morning, and we will see what we can do for you."

AND so it was that I started out early in the morning. I had put on a calico dress to work in and to suit my chosen trade. In a nice little bundle, covered with brown paper with a grease-spot on the center of it, was my lunch. I had an idea that every working girl carried a lunch, and I was trying to give out the impression that I was quite used to this thing. Indeed, I considered the lunch a telling stroke of thoughtfulness in my new *rôle*, and eyed with some pride, in which was mixed a little dismay, the grease-spot, which was gradually growing in size.

Early as it was, I found all the girls there and at work. I went through a small wagon-yard, the only entrance to the office. After making my excuses to the gentleman at the desk, he called to a pretty little girl, who had her apron full of pasteboard, and said:

"Take this lady up to Norah."

"Is she to work on boxes or cornucopias?" asked the girl.

"Tell Norah to put her on boxes."

Following my little guide, I climbed the narrowest, darkest, and most perpendicular stair it has ever been my misfortune to see. On and on we went, through small rooms filled with working girls, to the top floor — fourth or fifth story, I have forgotten which. Anyway, I was breathless when I got there.

"Norah, here is a lady you are to put on boxes," called out my pretty little guide.

All the girls that surrounded the long tables turned from their work and looked at me curiously. The auburn-haired girl addressed as Norah raised her eyes from the box she was making and replied:

"See if the hatchway is down and show her where to put her clothes."

Then the forewoman ordered one of the girls to "get the lady a stool," and sat down before a long table, on which was piled a lot of pasteboard squares, labeled in the center. Norah spread some long slips of paper on the table; then taking up a scrub-brush, she dipped it into a bucket of paste and then rubbed it over the paper. Next she took one of the squares of pasteboard and, running her thumb deftly along, turned up the edges. This done, she took one of the slips of paper and put it quickly and neatly over the corner, binding them together and holding them in place. She quickly cut the paper off at the edge with her thumb-nail and swung the thing around and did the next corner. This I soon found made a box lid. It looked and was very easy, and in a few moments I was able to make one.

I did not find the work difficult to learn, but rather disagreeable. The room was not ventilated, and the paste and glue were very offensive. The piles of boxes made conversation impossible with all the girls except a beginner, Therese, who sat by my side. She was very timid at first, but after I questioned her kindly, she grew more communicative.

"I live on Eldrige Street with my parents. My father is a musician, but he will not go on the streets to play. He very seldom gets an engagement. My mother is sick nearly all the time. I have a sister who works at *passementerie*. She can earn from $3 to $5 a week. I have another sister who has been spooling silk in Twenty-third Street for five years now. She makes $6 a week. When she comes home at night, her face and hands and hair are all colored from the silk she works on during the day. It makes her sick, and she is always taking medicine."

"Have you worked before?"

"Oh, yes; I used to work at *passementerie* on Spring Street. I worked from 7 until 6 o'clock, piecework, and made about $3.50 a week. I left because the bosses were not kind, and we only had three little oil lamps to see to work by. The rooms were very dark, but they never allowed us to burn the gas. Ladies used to come here and take the work home to do. They did it cheap, for the pleasure of doing it, so we did not get as much pay as we would otherwise."

"What did you do after you left there?" I asked.

"I went to work in a fringe factory on Canal Street. A woman had the place and she was very unkind to all the girls. She did not speak English. I worked an entire week, from 8 to 6, with only a half-hour for dinner, and at the end of the week she only paid me 35 cents. You know a girl cannot live on 35 cents a week, so I left."

"How do you like the box factory?"

"Well, the bosses seem very kind. They always say good-morning to me, a thing never done in any other place I ever worked, but it is a good deal for a poor girl to give two weeks' work for nothing. I have been here almost two weeks, and I have done a great deal of work. It's all clear gain to the bosses. They say they often dismiss a girl after her first two weeks on the plea that she does not suit. After this I am to get $1.50 a week."

WHEN the whistles of the surrounding factories blew at 12 o'clock, the forewoman told us we could quit work and eat our lunch. I was not quite so proud of my cleverness in simulating a working girl when one of them said:

"Do you want to send out for your lunch?"

"No; I brought it with me," I replied.

"Oh!" she exclaimed, with a knowing inflection and amused smile.

"Is there anything wrong?" I asked, answering her smile.

"Oh, no," quickly; "only the girls always make fun of any one who carries a basket now. No working-girl will carry a lunch or basket. It is out of style because it marks the girl at once as a worker. I would like to carry a basket, but I don't dare, because they would make so much fun of me."

The girls sent out for lunch and I asked of them the prices. For five cents they get a good pint of coffee, with sugar and milk if desired. Two cents will buy three slices of buttered bread. Three cents, a sandwich. Many times a number of the girls will put all their money together and buy quite a little food. A bowl of soup for five cents will give four girls a taste. By clubbing together they are able to buy warm lunch.

* * * *

AT one o'clock, we were all at work again. I — having completed sixty-four lids, and the supply being consumed — was put at "molding in." This is fitting the bottom into the sides of the box and pasting it there. It is rather difficult at first to make all the edges come closely and neatly together, but after a little experience, it can be done easily.

ON my second day, I was put at a table with some new girls, and I tried to get them to talk. I was surprised to find that they are very timid about telling their names, where they live, or how. I endeavored by every means a woman knows to get an invitation to visit their homes, but did not succeed.

"How much can girls earn here?" I asked the forewoman.

"I do not know," she said; "they never tell each other, and the bosses keep their time."

"Have you worked here long?" I asked.

"Yes, I have been here eight years, and in that time I have taught my three sisters."

"Is the work profitable?"

"Well, it is steady; but a girl must have many years' experience before she can work fast enough to earn much."

THE girls all seem happy. During the day, they would make the little building resound with their singing. A song would be begun on the second floor, probably, and each floor would take it up in succession, until all were singing. They were nearly always kind to one another. Their little quarrels did not last long, nor were they very fierce. They were all extremely kind to me and did all they could to make my work easy and pleasant. I felt quite proud when able to make an entire box.

There were two girls at one table on piecework who had been in a great many box factories and had had a varied experience.

"Girls do not get paid half enough at any work. Box factories are no worse than other places. I do not know anything a girl can do where by hard work she can earn more than $6 a week. A girl cannot dress and pay her boarding on that."

"Where do such girls live?" I asked.

"There are boarding-places on Bleecker and Houston, and around such places, where girls can get a room and meals for $3.50 a week. The room may be only for two, in one bed, or it may have a dozen, according to size. They have no conveniences or comforts, and generally undesirable men board at the same place."

"Why don't they live at these homes that are run to accommodate working women?"

"Oh, those homes are frauds. A girl cannot obtain any more home comforts, and then the restrictions are more than they will endure. A girl who works all day must have some recreation, and she never finds it in homes."

"Have you worked in box factories long?"

"For eleven years, and I can't say that it has ever given me a living. On an average, I make $5 a week. I pay out $3.50 for board, and my wash bill at the least is 75 cents. Can any one expect a woman to dress on what remains?"

"What do you get paid for boxes?"

"I get 50 cents a hundred for one-pound candy boxes, and 40 cents a hundred for half-pound boxes."

"What work do you do on a box for that pay?"

"Everything. I get the pasteboard cut in squares the same as you did. I first 'set up' the lids, then I 'mold in' the bottoms. This forms a box. Next I do the 'trimming,' which is putting the gilt edge around the box lid. 'Cover striping' (covering the edge of the lid) is next, and then comes the 'top label,' which finishes the lid entire. Then I paper the box, do the 'bottom labeling,' and then put in two or four laces (lace paper) on the inside as ordered. Thus you see one box passes through my hands eight times before it is finished. I have to work very hard and without ceasing to be able to make two hundred boxes a day, which earns me $1. It is not enough pay. You see, I handle two hundred boxes sixteen hundred times for $1. Cheap labor, isn't it?"

One very bright girl, Maggie, who sat opposite me, told a story that made my heart ache.

"This is my second week here," she said, "and, of course, I won't receive any pay until next week, when I expect to receive $1.50 for six days' work. My father was a driver before he got sick. I don't know what is wrong, but the doctor says he will die. Before I left this morning, he said my father will die soon. I could hardly work because of it. I am the oldest child, and I have a brother and two sisters younger. I am sixteen, and my brother is twelve. He gets $2 a week for being office-boy at a cigar-box factory."

"Do you have much rent to pay?"

"We have two rooms in a house on Houston Street. They are small and have low ceilings, and there are a great many Chinamen in the same house. We pay for these rooms $14 per month. We do not have much to eat, but then father doesn't mind it because he can't eat. We could not live if father's lodge did not pay our rent."

"Did you ever work before?"

"Yes, I once worked in a carpet factory at Yonkers. I only had to work there one week until I learned, and afterward I made at piecework a dollar a day. When my father got so ill, my mother wanted me at home, but now when we see I can earn so little, they wish I had remained there."

"Why do you not try something else?" I asked.

"I wanted to, but could find nothing. Father sent me to school until I was fourteen, and so I thought I would learn to be a telegraph operator. I went to a place in Twenty-third Street, where it is taught, but the man said he would not give me a lesson unless I paid fifty dollars in advance. I could not do that."

I then spoke of the Cooper Institute, which I thought every New Yorker knew was for the benefit of just such cases. I was greatly astonished to learn that such a thing as the Cooper Institute was wholly unknown to all the workers around me.

"If my father knew that there was a free school, he would send me," said one.

"I would go in the evenings," said another, "if I had known there was such a place."

Again, when some of them were complaining of unjust wages, and some of places where they had been unable to collect the amount due them after working, I spoke of the mission of the Knights of Labor, and the newly organized society for women. They were all surprised to hear that there were any means to aid women in having justice. I moralized somewhat on the use of any such societies unless they entered the heart of these factories.

One girl who worked on the floor below me said they were not allowed to tell what they earned. However, she had been working here five years, and she did not average more than $5 a week. The factory in itself was a totally unfit place for women. The rooms were small and there was no ventilation. If case of fire, there was practically no escape.

THE work was tiresome, and after I had learned all I could from the rather reticent girls, I was anxious to leave. I noticed some rather peculiar things on my trip to and from the factory. I noticed that men were much quicker to offer their places to the working-girls on the cars than they were to offer them to well-dressed women. Another thing quite as noticeable, I had more men try to get up a flirtation with me while I was a box-factory girl than I ever had before. The girls were nice in their manners and as polite as ones reared at home. They never forgot to thank one another for the slightest service, and there was quite a little air of "good form" in many of their actions. I have seen many worse girls in much higher positions than the white slaves of New York.

THE END

www.ingramcontent.com/pod-product-compliance
Lightning Source LLC
Chambersburg PA
CBHW050908120626
46554CB00003B/1086